Traditional Hymns

BOOK 1

Arranged by Fred Kern · Phillip Keveren · Mona Rejino

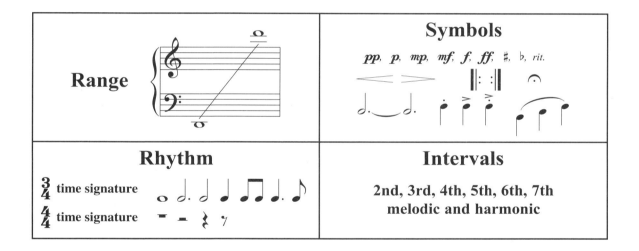

Range	Symbols
	pp, *p*, *mp*, *mf*, *f*, *ff*, ♯, ♭, *rit.*
Rhythm	**Intervals**
3/4 time signature 4/4 time signature	2nd, 3rd, 4th, 5th, 6th, 7th melodic and harmonic

ISBN 978-1-4234-8089-1

HAL•LEONARD®
CORPORATION
7777 W. BLUEMOUND RD. P.O. BOX 13819 MILWAUKEE, WI 53213

In Australia contact:
Hal Leonard Australia Pty. Ltd.
4 Lentara Court
Cheltenham, Victoria, 3192 Australia
Email: ausadmin@halleonard.com.au
Copyright © 2009 by HAL LEONARD CORPORATION
International Copyright Secured   All Rights Reserved

Visit Hal Leonard Online at
www.halleonard.com

Traditional Hymns

BOOK 1

Suggested Order of Study:

Deep and Wide

For the Beauty of the Earth

Jesus Loves Me

Amazing Grace

Faith of Our Fathers

Come, Christians, Join to Sing

All Glory, Laud and Honor

I Sing the Mighty Power of God

What a Friend We Have in Jesus

Now Thank We All Our God

O Worship the King

Joyful, Joyful, We Adore Thee

It Is Well with My Soul

A Mighty Fortress Is Our God

Holy, Holy, Holy! Lord God Almighty

Come, Thou Almighty King

 Full orchestral arrangements, included with this book on CD, may be used for both practice and performance. The enclosed audio CD is playable on any CD player. For Windows and Mac computer users, the CD is enhanced so you can access MIDI files for each song.

 TRACKS 9/10 The first track number is a practice tempo. The second track number is the performance tempo.

Contents

	Page	CD tracks

Deep and Wide

Amazing Grace

Words by John Newton From A Collection of Sacred Ballads
Traditional American Melody From Carrell and Clayton's Virginia Harmony
Arranged by Edwin O. Excell
Adapted by Mona Rejino

For the Beauty of the Earth

Words by Folliot S. Pierpoint
Music by Conrad Kocher
Arranged by Fred Kern

Accompaniment (Student plays one octave higher than written.) 🔘 **TRACKS 5/6**

Jesus Loves Me

Words by Anna B. Warner
Music by William B. Bradbury
Arranged by Fred Kern

Accompaniment (Student plays one octave higher than written.)   TRACKS 7/8

Faith of Our Fathers

Words by Frederick William Faber
Music by Henri F. Hemy and James G. Walton
Arranged by Mona Rejino

What a Friend We Have in Jesus

Words by Joseph M. Scriven
Music by Charles C. Converse
Arranged by Phillip Keveren

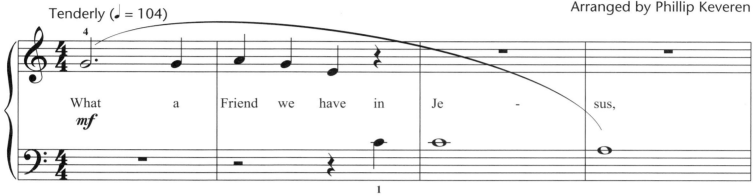

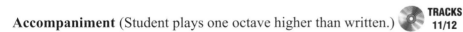

Accompaniment (Student plays one octave higher than written.) **TRACKS 11/12**

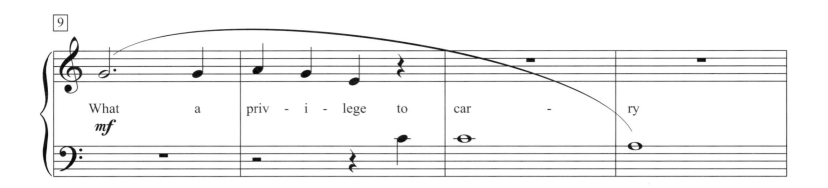

What a priv - i - lege to car - ry

mf

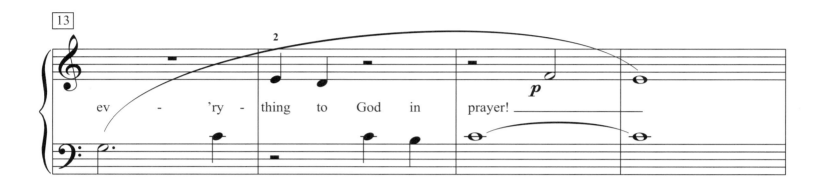

ev - 'ry - thing to God in prayer! _____

p

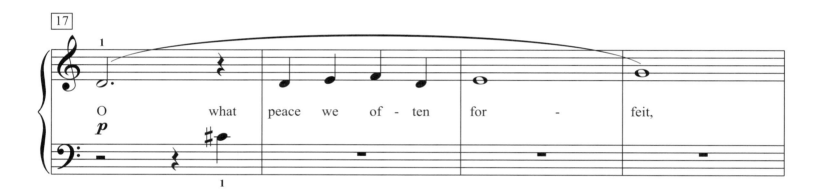

O what peace we of - ten for - feit,

p

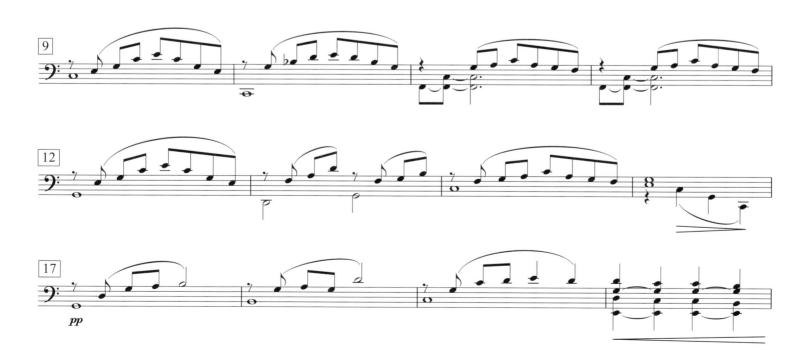

pp

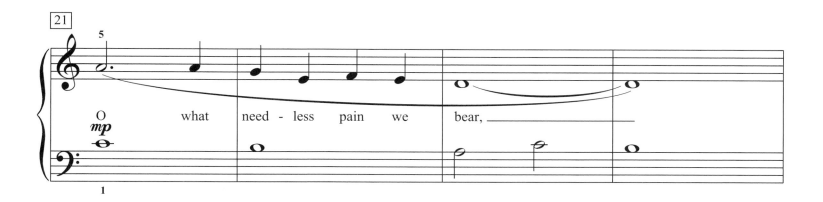

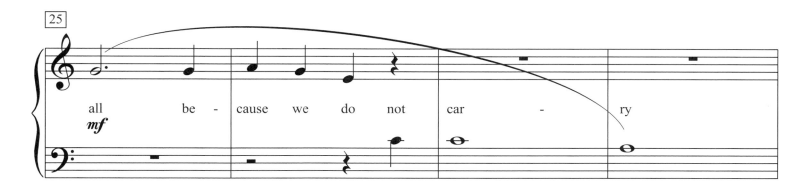

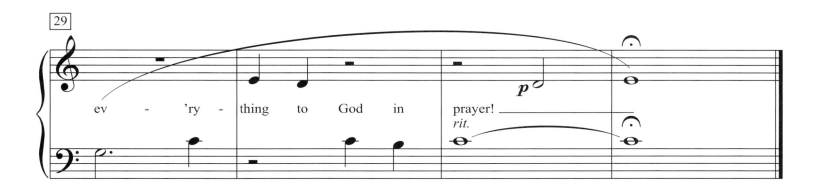

11

Come, Christians, Join to Sing

Words by Christian Henry Bateman
Traditional Spanish Melody
Arranged by Phillip Keveren

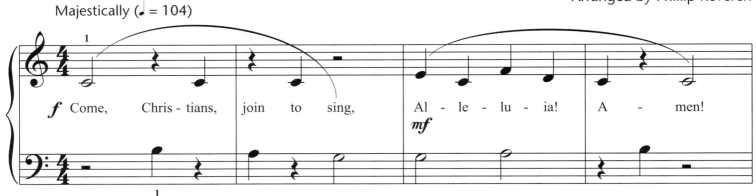

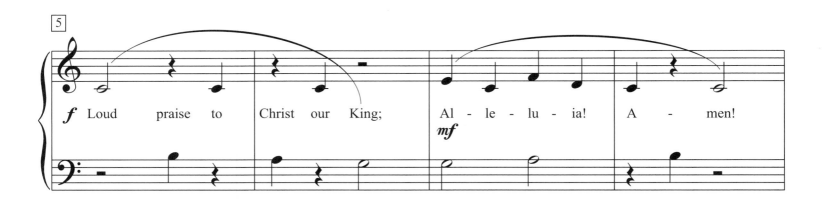

Accompaniment (Student plays one octave higher than written.) TRACKS 13/14

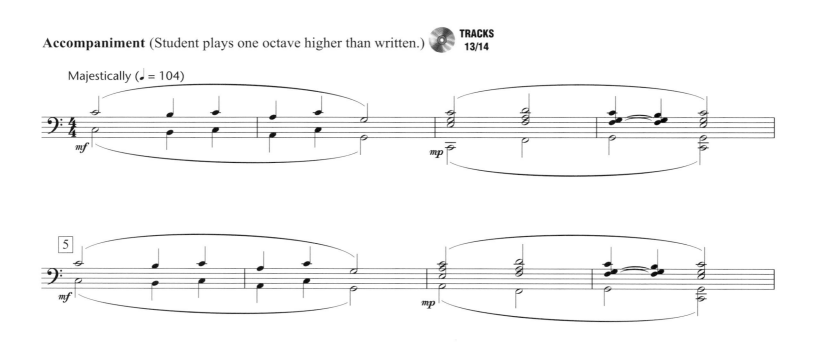

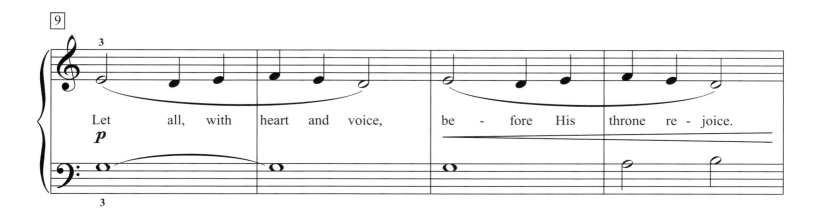

Let all, with heart and voice, be - fore His throne re - joice.

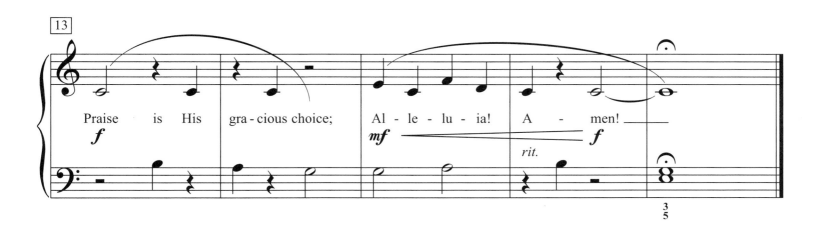

Praise is His gra - cious choice; Al - le - lu - ia! A - men!

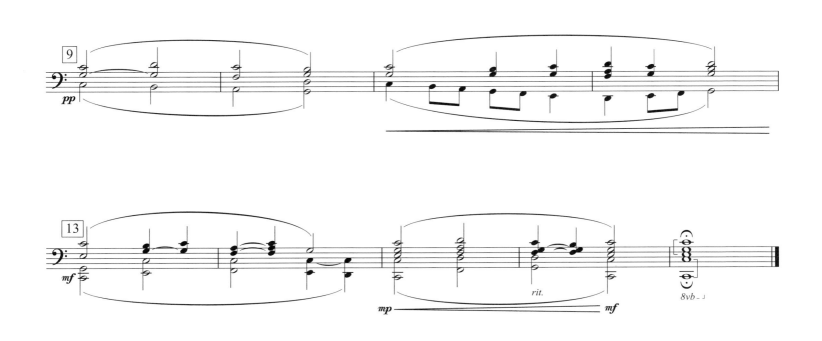

I Sing the Mighty Power of God

Words by Isaac Watts
Traditional English Melody
Arranged by Mona Rejino

With strength, in 'two' (♩ = 76)

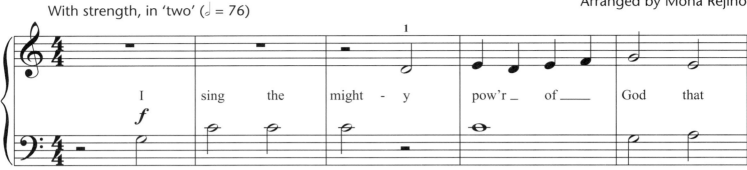

I sing the might-y pow'r of God that

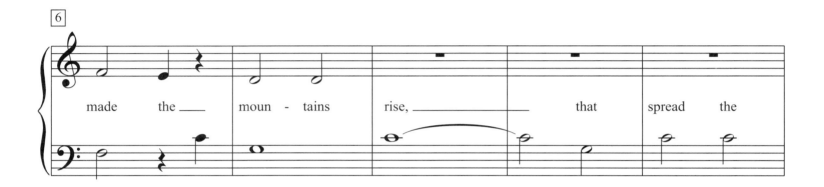

made the moun-tains rise, that spread the

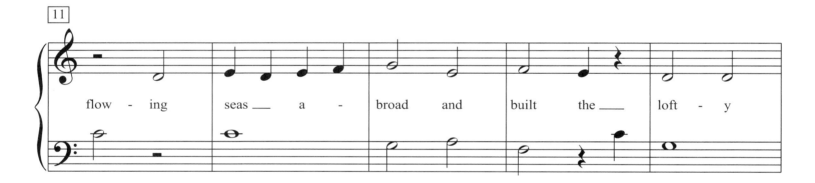

flow-ing seas a - broad and built the loft - y

Accompaniment (Student plays one octave higher than written.) 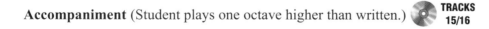 **TRACKS 15/16**

With strength, in 'two' (♩ = 76)

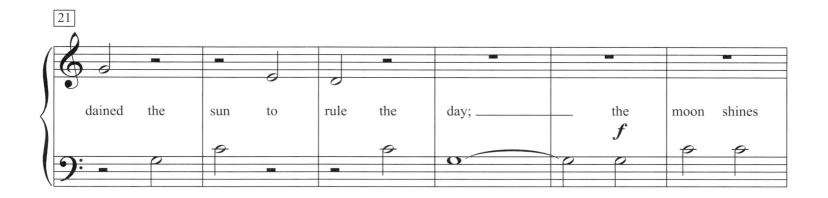

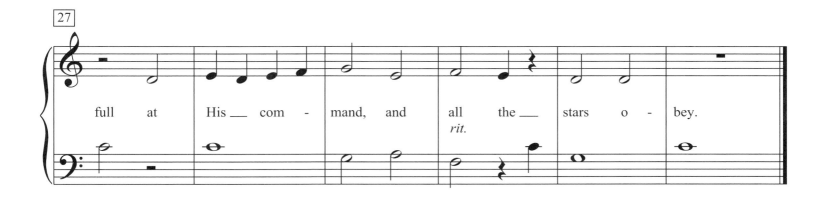

All Glory, Laud and Honor

Words by Theodulph of Orleans
Translated by John Mason Neale
Music by Melchior Teschner
Arranged by Fred Kern

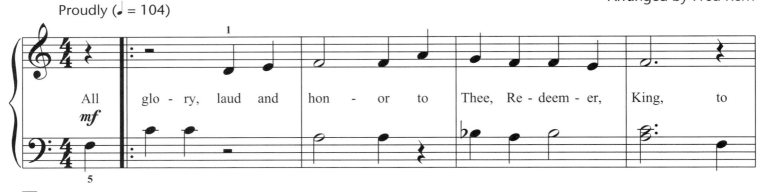

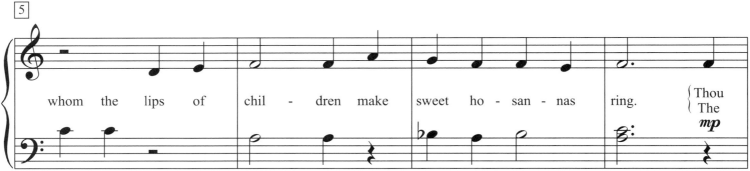

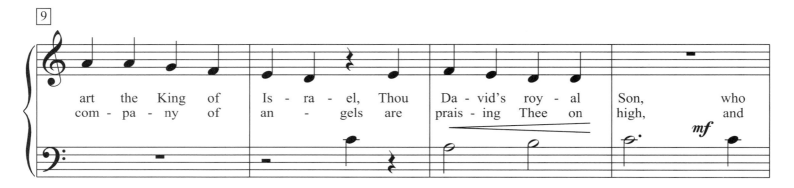

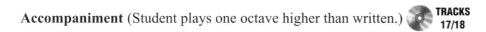

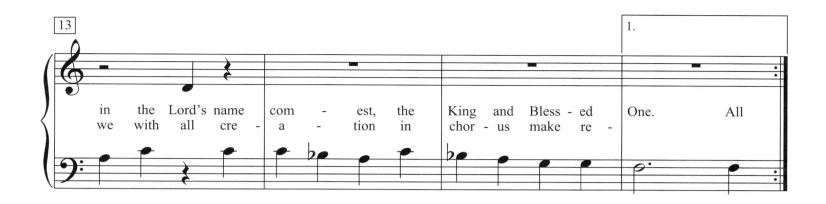

in the Lord's name com - est, the King and Bless - ed One. All
we with all cre - a - tion in chor - us make re -

ply. All glo - ry, laud and hon - or to Thee, Re - deem - er

King, to whom the lips of chil - dren make sweet ho - san - nas ring.

Now Thank We All Our God

German Words by Martin Rinkart
English Translation by Catherine Winkworth
Music by Johann Cruger
Arranged by Mona Rejino

Now thank we all our God with heart and hands and voic - es, who

won - drous things hath done, in whom His world re - joic - es; who,

Accompaniment (Student plays one octave higher than written.)

TRACKS
19/20

Moderately slow (♩ = 88)

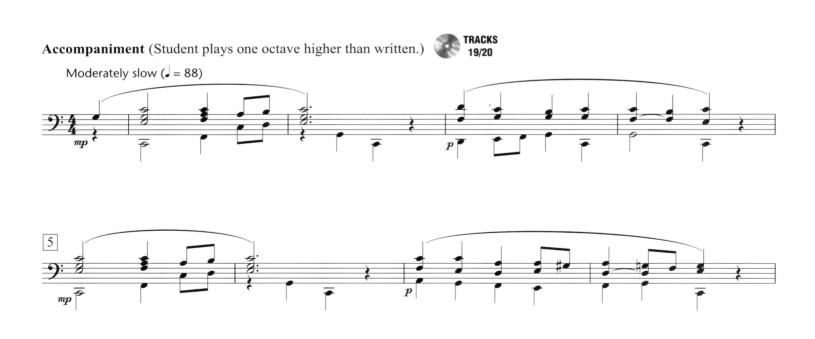

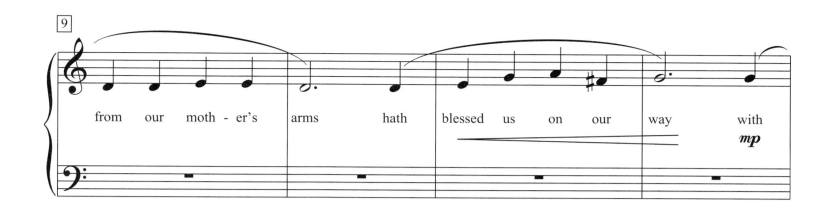

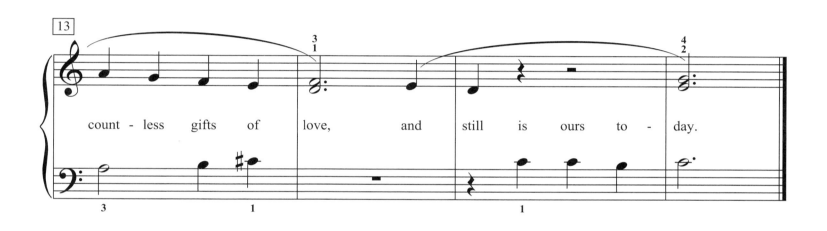

O Worship the King

Words by Robert Grant
Music attributed to Johann Michael Haydn
Arranged by Phillip Keveren

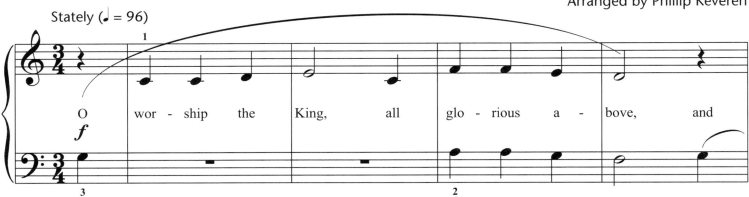

O wor-ship the King, all glo-rious a-bove, and

grate-ful-ly sing His won-der-ful love; our

Accompaniment (Student plays one octave higher than written.)

TRACKS
21/22

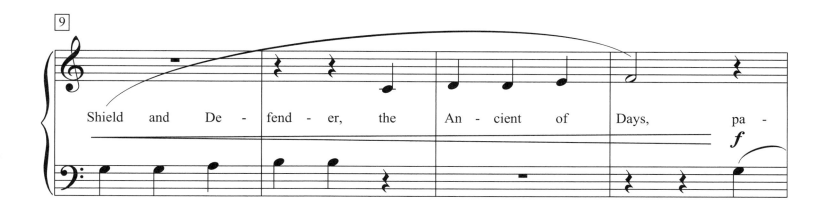

Shield and De - fend - er, the An - cient of Days, pa -

f

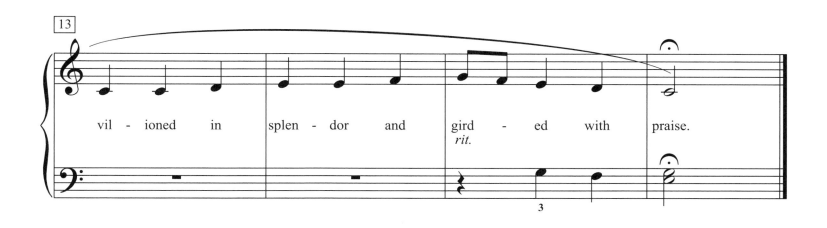

vil - ioned in splen - dor and gird - ed with praise.

rit.

pp cresc.

mf

rit.

Joyful, Joyful, We Adore Thee

Words by Henry van Dyke
Music by Ludwig van Beethoven, melody from *Ninth Symphony*
Adapted by Edward Hodges
Arranged by Fred Kern

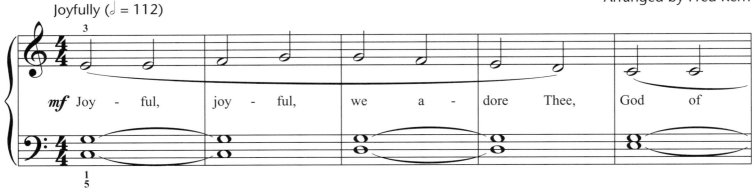

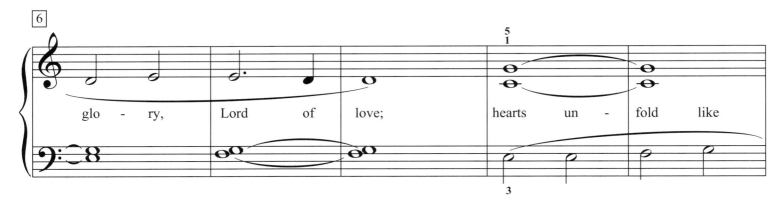

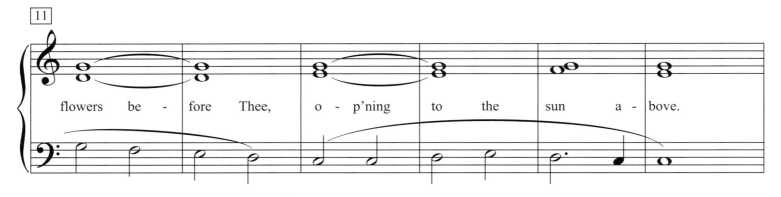

Accompaniment (Student plays one octave higher than written.)

TRACKS 23/24

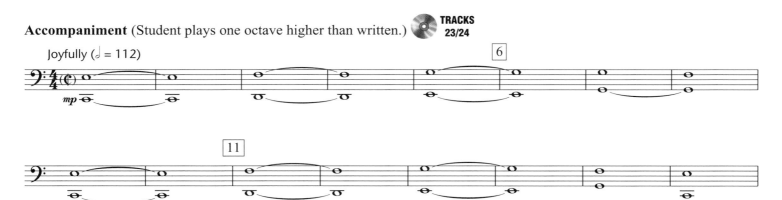

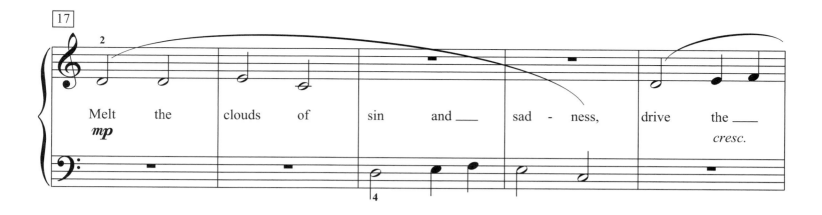

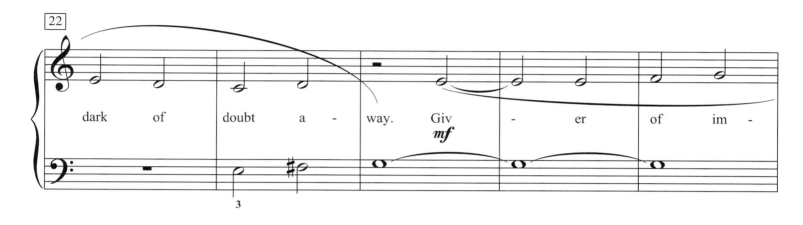

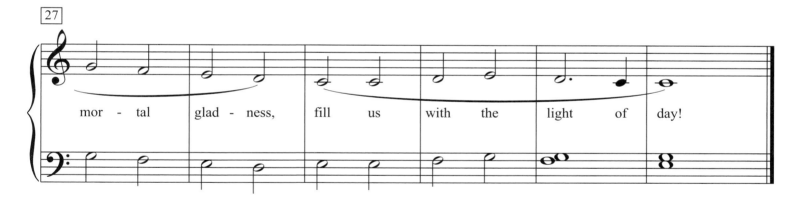

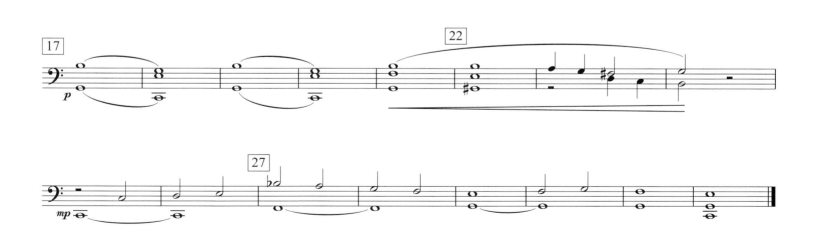

It Is Well with My Soul

Words by Horatio G. Spafford
Music by Philip P. Bliss
Arranged by Phillip Keveren

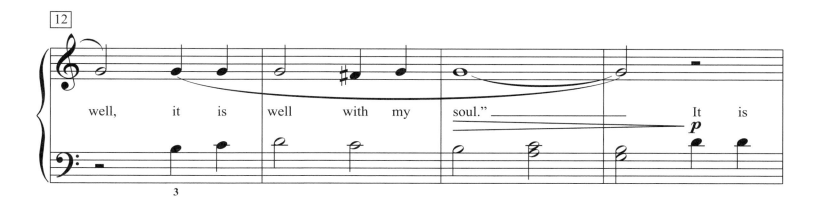

well, it is well with my soul." It is

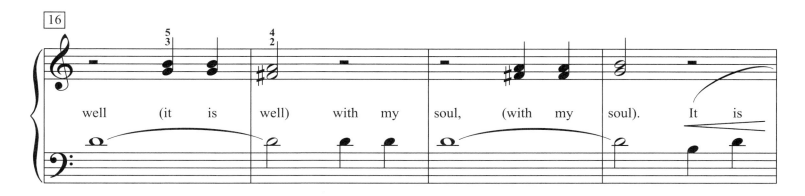

well (it is well) with my soul, (with my soul). It is

well, it is well with my soul.

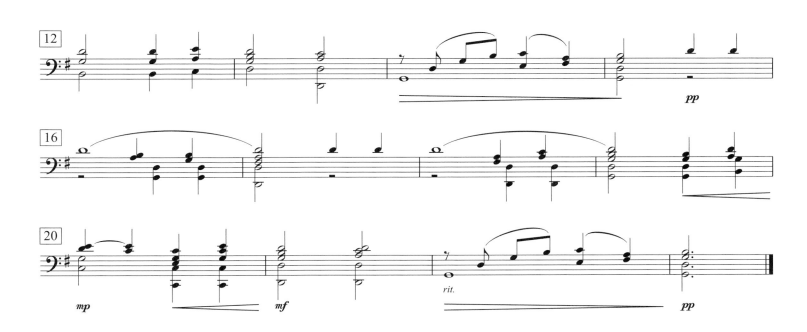

A Mighty Fortress Is Our God

Words and Music by Martin Luther
Translated by Frederick H. Hedge
Based on Psalm 46
Arranged by Fred Kern

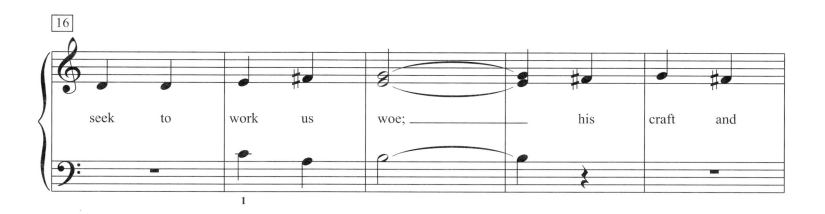

seek to work us woe; _____ his craft and

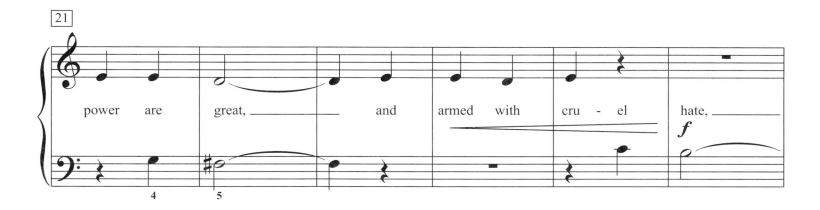

power are great, _____ and armed with cru - el hate, _____

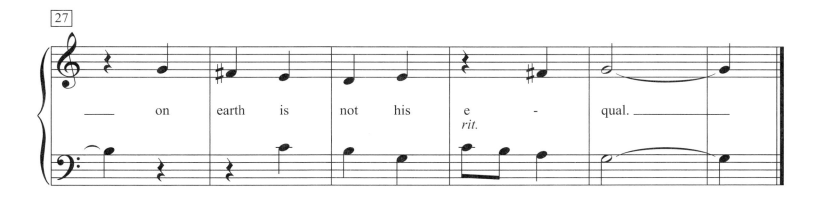

_____ on earth is not his e - qual. _____

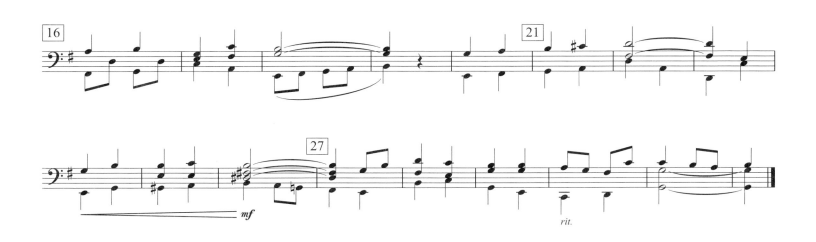

Holy, Holy, Holy! Lord God Almighty

Words by Reginald Heber
Music by John B. Dykes
Arranged by Mona Rejino

Come, Thou Almighty King

Traditional
Music by Felice de Giardini
Arranged by Fred Kern

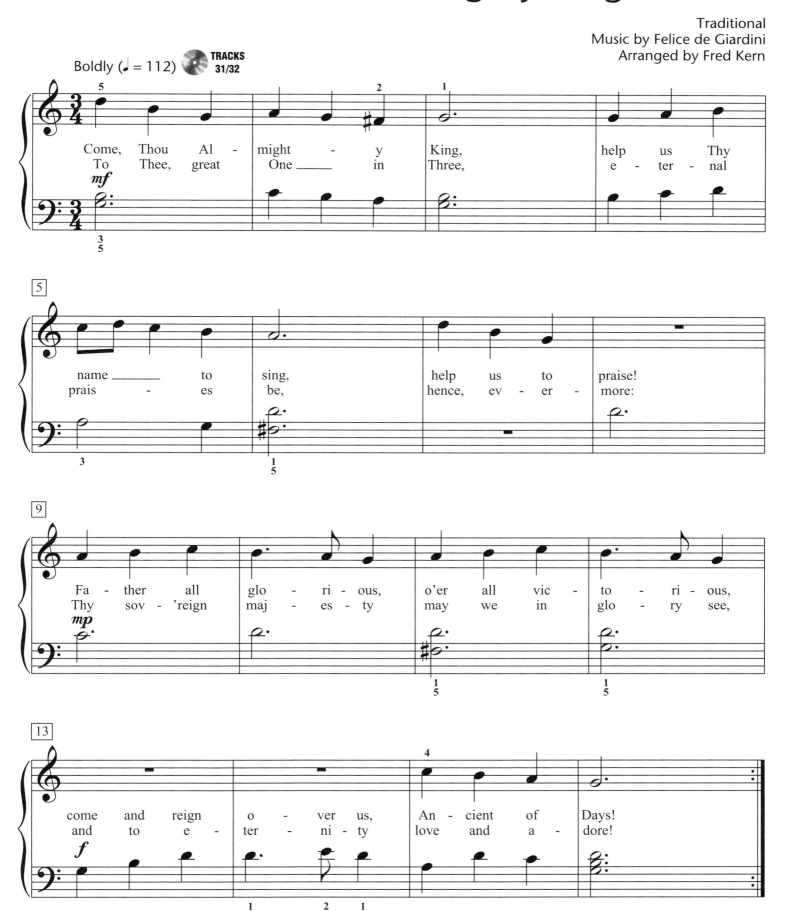

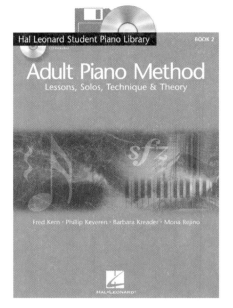

This series showcases the varied talents of our **Hal Leonard Student Piano Library** family of composers.

Here is where you will find great original piano music by your favorite composers, including Phillip Keveren, Carol Klose, Jennifer Linn, Bill Boyd, and many others. Carefully graded for easy selection, each book contains gems that are certain to become tomorrow's classics!

EARLY ELEMENTARY

JAZZ PRELIMS
by Bill Boyd
HL00290032　12 Solos.......................$5.95

ELEMENTARY

JAZZ STARTERS I
by Bill Boyd
HL00290425　10 Solos.......................$6.95

JUST PINK
by Jennifer Linn
HL00296722　9 Solos.......................$5.95

MUSICAL MOODS
by Phillip Keveren
HL00296714　7 Solos.......................$5.95

PUPPY DOG TALES
by Deborah Brady
HL00296718　5 Solos.......................$6.95

LATE ELEMENTARY

CIRCUS SUITE
by Mona Rejino
HL00296665　5 Solos.......................$5.95

CORAL REEF SUITE
by Carol Klose
HL00296354　7 Solos.......................$5.95

IMAGINATIONS IN STYLE
by Bruce Berr
HL00290359　7 Solos.......................$5.95

JAZZ STARTERS II
by Bill Boyd
HL00290434　11 Solos.......................$6.95

JAZZ STARTERS III
by Bill Boyd
HL00290465　12 Solos.......................$6.95

LES PETITES IMAGES
by Jennifer Linn
HL00296664　7 Solos.......................$6.95

MOUSE ON A MIRROR
by Phillip Keveren
HL00296361　5 Solos.......................$6.95

PLAY THE BLUES!
by Luann Carman (Method Book)
HL00296357　10 Solos.......................$8.99

SHIFTY-EYED BLUES
by Phillip Keveren
HL00296374　5 Solos.......................$6.95

TEX-MEX REX
by Phillip Keveren
HL00296353　6 Solos.......................$5.95

THROUGHOUT THE YEAR
by Christos Tsitsaros
HL00296723　12 Duets.......................$6.95

THE TOYMAKER'S WORKSHOP
by Deborah Brady
HL00296513　5 Duets.......................$5.95

TRADITIONAL CAROLS FOR TWO
arr. by Carol Klose
HL00296557　5 Duets.......................$7.99

EARLY INTERMEDIATE

DANCES FROM AROUND THE WORLD
by Christos Tsitsaros
HL00296688　7 Solos.......................$6.95

FANCIFUL WALTZES
by Carol Klose
HL00296473　5 Solos.......................$7.95

JAZZ BITS AND PIECES
by Bill Boyd
HL00290312　11 Solos.......................$6.95

MONDAY'S CHILD
by Deborah Brady
HL00296373　7 Solos.......................$6.95

PORTRAITS IN STYLE
by Mona Rejino
HL00296507　6 Solos.......................$6.95

THINK JAZZ!
by Bill Boyd (Method Book)
HL00290417.......................$9.95

THE TWELVE DAYS OF CHRISTMAS
arr. Deborah Brady
HL00296531　13 Solos.......................$6.95

WORLD GEMS
arr. Amy O'Grady (Piano Ens./2 Pianos, 8 Hands)
HL00296505　6 Folk Songs.................$6.95

INTERMEDIATE

AMERICAN IMPRESSIONS
by Jennifer Linn
HL00296471　6 Solos $7.95

ANIMAL TONE POEMS
by Michele Evans
HL00296439　10 Solos.......................$6.95

CHRISTMAS IMPRESSIONS
by Jennifer Linn
HL00296706　8 Solos.......................$6.95

CONCERTO FOR YOUNG PIANISTS
by Matthew Edwards (2 Pianos, 4 Hands)
HL00296356　Book/CD.....................$16.95

CONCERTO NO. 2 IN G MAJOR
by Matthew Edwards (2 Pianos, 4 Hands)
HL00296670　3 Movements.............$16.95

DAKOTA DAYS
by Sondra Clark
HL00296521　5 Solos.......................$6.95

DESERT SUITE
by Carol Klose
HL00296667　6 Solos.......................$6.95

For full descriptions and song lists for the books listed here, and to view a complete list of titles in this series, please visit our website at **www.halleonard.com**

Prices, contents, & availability subject to change without notice.

FOR MORE INFORMATION, SEE YOUR LOCAL MUSIC DEALER, OR WRITE TO:

HAL•LEONARD® CORPORATION
7777 W. BLUEMOUND RD. P.O. BOX 13819 MILWAUKEE, WI 53213

FAVORITE CAROLS FOR TWO
arr. Sondra Clark
HL00296530　5 Duets.......................$6.95

FLORIDA FANTASY SUITE
by Sondra Clark
HL00296766　3 Duets.......................$7.95

ISLAND DELIGHTS
by Sondra Clark
HL00296666　4 Solos.......................$6.95

JAMBALAYA
by Eugénie Rocherolle (2 Pianos, 8 Hands)
HL00296654　Piano Ensemble............$9.95

JAZZ DELIGHTS
by Bill Boyd
HL00240435　11 Solos.......................$6.95

JAZZ FEST
by Bill Boyd
HL00240436　10 Solos.......................$6.95

JAZZ MOODS
by Tony Caramia
HL00296728　8 Solos.......................$6.95

JAZZ SKETCHES
by Bill Boyd
HL00220001　8 Solos.......................$6.95

LES PETITES IMPRESSIONS
by Jennifer Linn
HL00296355　6 Solos.......................$6.95

MELODY TIMES TWO
arr. by Eugénie Rocherolle
HL00296360　4 Duets.......................$12.95

MONDAY'S CHILD
(A CHILD'S BLESSINGS)
by Deborah Brady
HL00296373　7 Solos.......................$6.95

POETIC MOMENTS
by Christos Tsitsaros
HL00296403　8 Solos.......................$7.95

ROMP!
by Phillip Keveren
(Digital Ensemble/6 Keyboards, 6 Players)
HL00296549　Book/CD.....................$9.95
HL00296548　Book/GM Disk $9.95

SONATINA HUMORESQUE
by Christos Tsitsaros
HL00296772　3 Movements...............$6.99

SONGS WITHOUT WORDS
by Christos Tsitsaros
HL00296506　9 Solos.......................$7.95

SUITE DREAMS
by Tony Caramia
HL00296775　4 Solos.......................$6.99

TALES OF MYSTERY
by Jennifer Linn
HL00296769　6 Solos.......................$7.99

THREE ODD METERS
by Sondra Clark (1 Piano, 4 Hands)
HL00296472　3 Duets $6.95

0109

POPULAR SONGS
HAL LEONARD STUDENT PIANO LIBRARY

The **Hal Leonard Student Piano Library** has great songs, and you will find all your favorites here: Disney classics, Broadway and movie favorites, and today's top hits. These graded collections are skillfully and imaginatively arranged for students and pianists at every level, from elementary solos with teacher accompaniments to sophisticated piano solos for the advancing pianist.

The Beatles
arr. Eugénie Rocherolle
Intermediate piano solos. Songs: *Can't Buy Me Love • Get Back • Here Comes the Sun • Martha My Dear • Michelle • Ob-La-Di, Ob-La-Da • Revolution • Yesterday.*
00296649 Correlates with HLSPL Level 5 ....$9.95

Broadway Hits
arr. Carol Klose
Early-Intermediate/Intermediate piano solos. Songs: *Beauty and the Beast • Circle of Life • Do-Re-Mi • It's a Grand Night for Singing • The Music of the Night • Tomorrow • Where Is Love? • You'll Never Walk Alone.*
00296650 Correlates with HLSPL Levels 4/5 ....$6.95

Chart Hits
arr. Mona Rejino
8 pop favorites carefully arranged at an intermediate level. Songs: *Bad Day • Boston • Everything • February Song • Home • How to Save a Life • Put Your Records On • What Hurts the Most.*
00296710 Correlates with HLSPL Level 5 ....$6.95

Christmas Cheer
arr. Phillip Keveren
Early Intermediate level. For 1 Piano/4 Hands. Songs: *Caroling, Caroling • The Christmas Song • It Must Have Been the Mistletoe • It's Beginning to Look like Christmas • Rudolph the Red-Nosed Reindeer • You're All I Want for Christmas.*
00296616 Correlates with HLSPL Level 4 ....$6.95

Christmas Time Is Here
arr. Eugénie Rocherolle
Intermediate level. For 1 piano/4 hands. Songs: *Christmas Time Is Here • Feliz Navidad • Here Comes Santa Claus (Right Down Santa Claus Lane) • I'll Be Home for Christmas • Little Saint Nick • White Christmas.*
00296614 Correlates with HLSPL Level 5 ....$6.95

Classic Joplin Rags
arr. Fred Kern
Intermediate/Late Intermediate. Six quintessential Joplin rags arranged by Fred Kern: *Bethena (Concert Waltz) • The Entertainer • Maple Leaf Rag • Pineapple Rag • Pleasant Moments (Ragtime Waltz) • Swipesy (Cake Walk).*
00296743 Correlates with HLSPL Level 5 ....$6.95

Disney Favorites
arr. Phillip Keveren
Late-Elementary/Early-Intermediate piano solos. Songs: *Beauty and the Beast • Circle of Life • A Dream Is a Wish Your Heart Makes • I'm Late; Little April Shower • A Whole New World (Aladdin's Theme) • You Can Fly! • You'll Be in My Heart.*
00296647 Correlates with HLSPL Levels 3/4 ....$9.95

Getting to Know You – Rodgers & Hammerstein Favorites
Illustrated music book. Elementary/Late Elementary piano solos with teacher accompaniments. Songs: *Bali H'ai • Dites-Moi (Tell Me Why) • The Farmer and the Cowman • Getting to Know You • Happy Talk • I Whistle a Happy Tune • I'm Gonna Wash That Man Right Outa My Hair • If I Loved You • Oh, What a Beautiful Mornin' • Oklahoma • Shall We Dance? • Some Enchanted Evening • The Surrey with the Fringe on Top.*
00296613 Correlates with HLSPL Level 3 ....$12.95

Elton John
arr. Carol Klose
8 classic Elton John songs arranged as intermediate solos: *Can You Feel the Love Tonight • Candle in the Wind • Crocodile Rock • Goodbye Yellow Brick Road • Sorry Seems to Be the Hardest Word • Tiny Dancer • Written in the Stars • Your Song.*
00296721 Correlates with HLSPL Level 5 ....$7.95

Jerome Kern Classics
arr. Eugénie Rocherolle
Intermediate level. Students young and old will relish these sensitive stylings of enduring classics: *All the Things You Are • Bill • Can't Help Lovin' Dat Man • I've Told Ev'ry Little Star • The Last Time I Saw Paris • Make Believe • Ol' Man River • Smoke Gets in Your Eyes • The Way You Look Tonight • Who?*
00296577 Correlates with HLSPL Level 5 ....$12.95

Melody Times Two
Classic Counter-Melodies for Two Pianos, Four Hands
arr. Eugénie Rocherolle
This collection of classic counter-melody songs features four elegant and thoroughly entertaining arrangements for two pianos, four hands. Includes a definition and history of counter-melodies throughout musical periods; song histories; and composer biographies. The folio includes two complete scores for performance. Intermediate Level 4 Duos: *Baby, It's Cold Outside • Play a Simple Melody • Sam's Song • (I Wonder Why?) You're Just in Love.*
00296360 Intermediate Duets $12.95

Movie Favorites
arr. Fred Kern
Early-Intermediate/Intermediate piano solos. Songs: *Forrest Gump (Feather Theme) • Hakuna Matata • My Favorite Things • My Heart Will Go On • The Phantom of the Opera • Puttin' On the Ritz • Stand by Me.*
00296648 Correlates with HLSPL Levels 4/5 ....$6.95

Sounds of Christmas (Volume 3)
arr. Rosemary Barrett Byers
Late Elementary/Early Intermediate level. For 1 piano/4 hands. Songs: *Blue Christmas • Christmas Is A-Comin' (May God Bless You) • I Saw Mommy Kissing Santa Claus • Merry Christmas, Darling • Shake Me I Rattle (Squeeze Me I Cry) • Silver Bells.*
00296615 Correlates with HLSPL Levels 3/4 ....$6.95

Today's Hits
arr. Mona Rejino
Intermediate-level piano solos. Songs: *Bless the Broken Road • Breakaway • Don't Know Why • Drops of Jupiter (Tell Me) • Home • Listen to Your Heart • She Will Be Loved • A Thousand Miles.*
00296646 Correlates with HLSPL Level 5 ....$6.95

You Raise Me Up
arr. Deborah Brady
Contemporary Christian favorites. Elementary-level arrangements. Optional teacher accompaniments add harmonic richness. Songs: *All I Need • Forever • Open the Eyes of My Heart, Lord • We Bow Down • You Are So Good to Me • You Raise Me Up.*
00296576 Correlates with HLSPL Levels 2/3 ....$7.95

FOR MORE INFORMATION, SEE YOUR LOCAL MUSIC DEALER,
OR WRITE TO:

HAL•LEONARD®
CORPORATION
7777 W. BLUEMOUND RD. P.O. BOX 13819 MILWAUKEE, WI 53213

Prices, contents and availability subject to change without notice.
Prices may vary outside the U.S.

Disney characters and artwork © Disney Enterprises, Inc.

0109

Visit our web site at **www.halleonard.com/hlspl.jsp**
for all the newest titles in this series
and other books in the Hal Leonard Student Piano Library.